Paradise

Paradise

Poems by Stephen Gibson

The University of Arkansas Press
Fayetteville
2011

ISBN-10: 1-55728-959-X
ISBN-13: 78-1-55728-959-9

15   14   13   12   11   5   4   3   2   1

Text design by Ellen Beeler

⊗ The paper used in this publication meets the minimum requirements of the
American National Standard for Permanence of Paper for Printed Library Materials
Z39.48-1984.

Library of Congress Cataloging-in-Publication Data

Gibson, Stephen, 1948-
  Paradise : poems / by Stephen Gibson.
    p. cm.
  ISBN-13: 978-1-55728-959-9 (pbk. : alk. paper)
  ISBN-10: 1-55728-959-X (pbk. : alk. paper)
  I. Title.
  PS3557.I225P37 2011
  811'.54--dc22

                                                      2010046106

Once again, for my wife Clo, my daughter Kyla,
and my son Joe

And also in memory of my mother Mary Agnes
and my father Russell

Acknowledgments

Some of the poems in this collection, or earlier versions of them, originally appeared in the following publications, and grateful acknowledgments are made to their editors: "Almonds" (forthcoming), *Alimentum;* "Memorial Sonnet," "Ghosts" ("It's funny how an object can become a person"), *Field;* "Ghazal" ("Decades ago, when Philippe Petit strung that tightrope between"), "Ghazal on a Panel of an Early Renaissance Triptych," *Margie;* "Masaccio's *The Expulsion of Adam and Eve from the Garden*," *Mid-American Review;* "Nighthawks," *New Delta Review;* "Sonnet for Auden" (forthcoming), *New York Quarterly;* "Life Study," *Ploughshares;* "Duomo and Baptistery, Florence," "Ghazal for Pretty Women and Venice," *River Styx.*

"Altichiero's Frescoes: The St. Catherine Cycle" originally appeared in *New Madrid* Summer 2009. "Details from Guido Reni's *Slaughter of the Innocents*," "Head Games," and "Fur" originally appeared in *New Madrid* Summer 2010.

Thanks to Barbara Hamby, David Kirby, and R. T. Smith for their generosity and support.

Finally, a special thanks to Enid Shomer for her care, time, and wonderful suggestions in editing this collection.

Contents

Duomo and Baptistery, Florence   3

Framed Photo of Venice Overlooking St. Mark's Square   6

Alberto Giacometti's *Woman with Her Throat Cut*   8

Memorial Sonnet   9

Ghosts   10

Masks   11

Memento Mori   13

Ghazal   16

Ghazal on a Panel of an Early Renaissance Triptych   17

Daedalus Presents the Artificial Cow to Pasiphae   18

Sonnet for Auden   19

Altichiero's Frescoes: The St. Catherine Cycle   20

At a Café in Venice   25

Details from Guido Reni's *Slaughter of the Innocents*   27

Masaccio's *The Expulsion of Adam and Eve from the Garden*   29

Piazza Shelley   31

Life Study   32

Head Games   33

Almonds   34

Fur   35

Brunelleschi's Dome   37

Faces   38

Ghazal   39

Nighthawks   40

Ghazal on NYPD Crime Scene Photos   41

Ghazal on a 1906 Murder Victim Photo   42

Ghazal on a 1914 NYC Crime Scene Photo   43

Ghazal on a 1910 NYC Crime Scene Photo   44

Ghazal on a 1912 NYC Crime Scene Photo   45

Ghazal on a 1916 Brooklyn Murder Scene Photo   46

Ghazal on a 1902 NYC Crime Scene Photo   47

Ghazal on a 1915 NYC Crime Scene Photo of a Couple   48

Ghazal on a 1909 NYC Crime Scene Photo   49

Ghazal on a 1908 Murder Victim Photo   50

Ghazal on a 1918 Murder Victim Photo   51

Ghazal for Pretty Women and Venice   52

Impromptu on Titian's *Annunciation*   54

Landscape with the Rape of Europa   56

Ghosts   57

Paradise

Duomo and Baptistery, Florence

I

A beautiful girl in a peasant skirt
      and blouse has taken a seat on the cathedral
steps, and it's impossible to avert

one's eyes from between the girl's
      legs. It's not just some old men staring—
so are women. One woman's mouth curls

and her lips pinch as if she's tasting
      something unpleasant, something sour
like a lemon, and the acid stings:

the girl's not wearing panties. She's bare
      all the way up to that irresistible darkness.
The men pretend not to look there

as they walk by her, slowly, and pass
      each other with a nod, as if their "secret"
weren't known, or their indifference

when they just happen to let
      their eyes wander in the same direction,
away from Ghiberti's bronze statuettes

which are not the real doors, but imitations.

II

Michelangelo was so stunned by their beauty,
        a tour guide says to a group in German,
then in French and English, *that he*

named them the Gates of Paradise. The man
        looks over at me because I'm not with the tour,
then turns back to the bronze where *Adam*

is raised from dust by his God in the door's
        first panel. On the lower right of that same panel,
Adam is seen sleeping on the garden floor

as Eve rises from his ribs. You can tell
        that mankind is still in a state of innocency
because if you look here Adam's genitals

are not hidden: he lies on his side and he
        faces us, asleep, while Eve is held up by angels—
these four cherubs—which pagan Romans called putti—

and which I've recorded to replay in my hotel.

III

Across the street from the white
        and green and pink marble of the Duomo
a young woman holds a jar of cellulite

cream in a large pharmacy window
    next to a display of Kodak film and batteries.
The cardboard model's back is turned to

us, so we see just part of her pouty
    and disapproving look as she stares down
at her bare behind. The model's body,

of course, is flawless, but her frown
    is supposed to suggest to other women
that she too has issues like their own

and the cream will solve their problem:
    at right, in a comic magnified close-up bubble
of her behind, there's the "before" skin

without the cream, adjacent to the beautiful.

IV

These doors are replicas. Only when she
    tucks in her skirt do the men look away from her,
truly disappointed, not only by what she

has done, but by everything, as if all were replicas.

Framed Photo of Venice Overlooking St. Mark's Square

for Tim

The gift my brother sent me arrived damaged.
        There was glass embedded in the mat,
and most of the tiny people posing

on St. Mark's balcony were cut in half or
        had their limbs detached or their heads
cut off. Mentally, I made a connection

to Iraq—this was July 2005—a connection
        that was circumstantial, and false. The damage
over there was real: real video of beheaded

workers whose backs were used as placemats
        for their heads, their bodies on dirty floors,
their faces turned to cameras, posing

for the Web, which I'd watched, interposing
        between them and me no connection;
my anonymous darkness and that floor

had no connection, and whatever damage
        this war was doing, wasn't in my name. (In my head
I knew this wasn't true, but that idea, like matte

glass, blurred everything). The mat
      of the photo was gouged, and tourists posing
below in St. Mark's Square had heads

floating off of shoulders; again, no connection
      to anything actual. Still, I'd seen damage.
Either the war on television was real, or

it wasn't: the bandages, the floors
      douched with buckets, mosques, prayer mats,
our soldiers, explosions. Either the damage

was actual, or it wasn't. Those families posing
      before St. Mark's had absolutely no connection
to real life; they were images. The child's head

floating off of his tiny shoulders, headed
      like a balloon to the top of St. Mark's, or
beyond, into the clouds, had no connection

to real life. It was an image. But it didn't matter.
      Like a piece of found art, this accidental imposing
of one meaning onto another pointed to damage.

I used tweezers to pick slivers from the mat, my head
      bending almost to St. Mark's floor, where families posing
for a photograph made an anonymous connection to all damage.

Alberto Giacometti's *Woman with Her Throat Cut*

It's a sculpture in the Peggy Guggenheim Museum in Venice.
I knew a woman whose husband beat her like this

and, so it wouldn't show, jab his thumbs under her armpits.
This one's made of metal and its throat's been slit.

I think sometimes he wanted to slit hers. He'd grasp
her throat, squeezing his thumb and fingers till she gasped

and with the other hand pulled down the shade as he warned her
she better not scream. I think you see that in the sculpture—

the scream that doesn't make a sound but is still
a scream. What's amazing is to see it both in flesh *and* metal.

At the same time, he wants her. That's why she's opening her legs
to him—she's hoping he won't cut her throat, so she begs

him to fuck her by lying on her back with her legs spread.
Both the man and woman I was thinking of are long dead.

Memorial Sonnet

This is for the bruised eye, the swollen lip,
the blue panties torn at the elastic,
the bra cup hanging out of the laundry basket
and the yellowing half slip

almost as yellowed as the girdle.
This is for the intentional cosmic
silence that watched like Sputnik
overhead and heard her yell.

This is for his psychiatric hospital visits
and her court-appointed lawyer;
this is for the restraining order
whenever he ignored it.

This is for my mother cowering in a corner.
This is for my father who came home from war.

Ghosts

It's funny how an object can become a person,
or the person an object, and both you fill up with all
sorts of things, which are important for some reason.

Like my deceased father's old suitcase—I'm his son,
but what I knew about him was locked inside a hall
closet. It's funny how an object can become a person.

I'd take the key from the handle and ask permission
before opening the locks. "Is that okay?" I'd call
out loud. That was important for some reason.

Of course, no one answered, and I figured if anyone
had a right to look, I did. Everything about him was all
in there. It's funny how an object can become the person.

I'd stare at the tiny handwriting in his V-mail—in one,
there was a photograph of him posing with his rifle
(his name on back, that was important for some reason)—

and I'd also wonder about who took the picture: the sun
was behind him, and, of course, you couldn't see him at all,
just his shadow, so the shadow had become the person.
I don't know why, but that was important for some reason.

Masks

Rome

1.

Outside the window at the Spanish Steps
a wedding party has assembled in front of the fountain—
bride, groom, a videographer's assistant who keeps

the chaos organized and reports back to him.
Of course, I can't hear them. I'm watching
from a window of the Keats-Shelley museum

where I've just looked at a pencil drawing
Severn did of Keats during the night he died
(Keats's hair is matted to his forehead; he'd been sweating).

The museum's young female assistant has tried
very hard to get me to understand (she's German)
everything I look at. When she's satisfied,

she keeps quiet while I stare, and she stands
next to me until I'm ready to move on. She watches
me, anticipating the body language of some man

she doesn't know. A minute ago, she was talking with such
passion about Keats's death mask inside its glass case
when a boom box outside began blasting a wedding march.

2.

It's hard to tell from the window what's real or isn't
since everything below is staged—the stationary horse
hasn't lifted one hoof from the plaza, and its bent

head hasn't moved. The bridal coach it's harnessed
to could be papier-mâché if the young couple inside
weren't leaning out of its windows. I think what's worse

is not knowing what's real, period. The bed Keats died
on, whose crumpled sheets and striped worn-out pillowcase
I stared at as if he still lay there (that I went teary-eyed

over), turned out to be a copy. So was the death mask.
Some of the letters displayed in the cases are genuine,
but others are facsimiles. Because of Keats's tuberculosis,

the authorities burned everything that belonged to him,
though Severn lied to them. There's much here that's for show—
not like in the gift shop (T-shirts with Grecian urns on them)—

but it's hard to know what's genuine. I'm at a window
staring at a bridal couple inside Cinderella's coach,
and the couple might really be in love for all I know.

Memento Mori

Florence

I

I've walked each morning to the Duomo
        as if on some mission from my hotel
on the Via Caponi, where my window

looks out onto a courtyard of other hotel
        windows—on each side a wall of windows,
sometimes with people, as if lining a well

that sinks down to restaurant trash bins below
        and a dog walk (I won't call it a garden)
where every once in a while, in shadows,

someone (most often it's been a woman)
        waits under a filthy green-and-white awning
for a dog to do its business and to then

come back—at least, that's the plan—but the thing
        never follows the plan, and I've seen the person
have to quickly step from under the awning

to threaten the dog for it to return, and only then.

II

At breakfast this morning, the old couple
     loaded their paper napkins with hard-boiled
eggs (brown, not white), cheese wedges, and hard rolls.

Once, I mistook them for a gay couple,
     but I haven't mistaken them for the same sex
since the time I watched him offer her a gold-foiled

packet of butter, and she politely refused it.
     I ran across them today in a hall of the Bargello
where I'd gone to see its famous miniature bronzes,

but I kept returning through the main hall
     to the family della Robbia's enameled terra cotta
reliefs. I followed the reliefs around the wall

and was surprised to see the couple just standing there,
     staring, not at Luca's joyful *Madonna of the Apple*
where the Christ toddler offers the fruit to his mother—

but at Andrea Robbia's *Portrait of a Lady*, a girl's
     high relief done so realistically that if you saw
the teenager you'd recognize her, the fifteenth-century enamel

peeling from her upper lip like a canker.

III: Coda

I went up to it: not like a canker—a kissing sore—
      a teen who's picked out lovely pearls, is conscious
her hair should fall just so above her shoulders,

and is so eager to live, she hasn't time for us.

Ghazal

Decades ago, when Philippe Petit strung that tightrope between
        the Twin Towers, life could surprise you in a blink in that city—

or in a Bronx apartment where my brother and I carried a piano
        up five flights, because sometimes you didn't think in that city,

you just did it. In front was the street; in back, an alley with clotheslines—
        a lot of girls washed their bras and panties in the sink in that city.

During the summer that Berkowitz heard that dog speak to him,
        some of those girls were lying on beach towels turning pink in
        that city,

and some were there when the planes hit—my brother won't talk
        about that, like he'll talk about using my draft card to drink in
        the city.

Ghazal on a Panel of an Early Renaissance Triptych

tempera on wood, fourteenth century, anonymous

Christ, like a cast member fill-in, saucer-eyed,
floats on invisible wires, a mountain ledge below him,

as scorched, still-smoking, bat-flapping, creosote Satan,
blown in from a blast furnace, hovers nearby, and shows him

a valley—down there, like a boxful of petit fours
and chocolate ovals, houses instantly appear below him.

The unknown artist's technique is primitive, and simple—
the temptation isn't: the choices Satan aims to bestow on him

will be limited only by desire: to want to be invisible, or peek
under a bathroom stall, or do threesomes, and no one will know him.

Daedalus Presents the Artificial Cow to Pasiphae

not exactly the myth

The barn exists somewhere. It could be in Sweden
because a Dutch porn site identifies that link.
Pasiphae, naked, washes between her legs at a sink
and stares out of a window. There are no men
anywhere. The barn's open doors invite her in,
though she is standing stock still at the sink
and has stopped washing herself. We think
the camera will pan down, but we're mistaken—
instantly, we're inside the barn with her:
the white bull does not look at all like a god
and the sleazy-looking man, not Daedalus,
holds fast to a rope leash. He stares out at us
as the woman positions herself on straw
under the bull, and gets it hard.

Sonnet for Auden

I don't remember if I met W. H. Auden
before or after this happened, but he
was on television, some special on public TV,
and my family was living in the Bronx then,
and I was a teen starting to write poetry.
I wrote on lined yellow paper, and in pen.
The poems weren't good, but my girlfriend
liked them, especially the love poems; she
thought "thou" was perfectly acceptable in
love poems, even though Auden had written
back on one of mine that it might not be—
we were alone, watching him on television,
and my girl, adamant, said lovers could
do anything. I think Auden understood.

Altichiero's Frescoes: The St. Catherine Cycle

Oratory of St. George, Padua

(i) St. Catherine Declares Her Christianity to the Pagans

At lower left a calf's throat is being slit.
The image is so tucked into the corner
of the fresco that a tourist watching her
might not notice. I know I didn't see it
when I first entered the chapel to look
around before I went back to buy a ticket.
The girl behind the counter fumbled, and it
occurred to me it was because of the book
she was reading. She hadn't seen me
come in, nor heard me until I spoke to her.
She thrust the paperback under a newspaper.
The cover was like something out of the 1950s
with a blonde junkie tying off her arm
as cops kick in the door. I meant no harm.

(ii) St. Catherine Converts Many of the Pagans

Altichiero's fresco powders from the wall.
What remains in place is held with copper pins.
In this scene, nothing will stop Catherine
from arguing her faith to Muslim infidels.
In the background, powerful men arrive
to keep an eye on her from their balcony.
The fresco's damage is severe, but you see
what happens to converts—they're burned alive.
I want to say something about the irony
of all this, something about the historical,
but there's no one here, and the girl just
wants to get back to reading. On the wall,
Catherine is still preaching, but she's
surrounded by ghost figures, and dust.

(iii) St. Catherine's Followers Renounce Their Faith

These women haven't vanished. They're
kneeling, burning incense to idols,
saying what powerful men tell
them to say. They've had their hair
piled up under white head scarves,
so they know what can happen next.
Altichiero emphasizes their long necks
by having them face the guy who carves
at the animal's throat. Behind the altar,
he pins the calf down, its wet tongue
licks air, his knee presses into its shoulder,
and his left hand pulls up at the jaw
as the blade enters. These young
women know that might be them, or her.

(iv) St. Catherine Miraculously Saved from the Torturer's Wheel

Suffering continues. Torturers torture,
victims suffer—but here, at least, the wheel
has stopped, and it is not because any feel
pity on the woman. They would break her
if they could, break every limb to prove
her wrong, snap every tendon in her until
none is left and they've all had their fill
of pain. But the apparatus won't move.

That's the miracle. They can do nothing.
The apparatus has broken, and her torturers
have fallen back as if struck by lightning—
they're that astonished. In the fresco, they stare
at her as if they see god inside the human being
when, of course, they don't—they'll behead her.

(v) St. Catherine Kneels before Her Executioner

He raises his sword. It's the moment of high
drama before the woman will crumple
into martyrdom, and her example
will inspire relic hunters. Next door, I
saw the lower jaw, larynx, and tongue
of St. Anthony displayed in reliquaries.
People were taping newspaper obituaries
to his altar, which showed many young,
smiling faces in their "before" pictures.
Several old women wept and kissed
the black marble, while others left letters
whose handwriting was blurred and smeared.
I felt embarrassed. I'm not a believer.
Catherine waits for the blow that won't miss.

At a Café in Venice

Near my table outside at a café next
to the Clock Tower in St. Mark's Square,
this guy was holding up the *New York Times,*
reading about the war, putting his cigarette
down to pick up his coffee cup, the newspaper
almost always kept in front of his face,

while I sat nearby watching his face,
hidden but saying *fuck,* and the next
second another *fuck,* the newspaper
shaking in his hands while in the square
tourists walked by him as his cigarette
went up to his mouth again each time

he put the coffee cup down, as each time
the cup replaced the cigarette at his face—
fuck—the newspaper shaking, the cigarette
in the tiny metal ashtray until his next
drag on it, the same tiny metal square
ashtray like the one on my table, his paper

Cinzano tablecloth just like my paper
Cinzano tablecloth, only this time
I had decided to eat because the square
wasn't too crowded, and every face
wasn't desperately searching for the next
table, or waiting for the last cigarette

on a table to be dumped with the cigarettes
on another table into a balled-up paper
tablecloth being replaced for the next
customer. So I decided to eat this time,
and then, finally, clearly, I saw the guy's face
because he folded the newspaper into a square

and stared down at it—Iraq, some square
with a charred corpse in it, a cigarette
stuck to some onlooker's mouth, his face
dumbfounded, frozen, staring at the newspaper
photographer for a photo to be in the *New York Times.*
When the guy left, I grabbed it before the next

customer sat. That's what it showed: a square the newspaper
wrote about this time with some guy with a cigarette
frozen to his face, wondering what would come next.

Details from Guido Reni's *Slaughter of the Innocents*

Vatican Museum

Unlike some war footage, this artist
doesn't turn away: one infant
is pinned, the sword all the way through
as the soldier looks behind him for release.
Who will gag the mother or tear off
her arms so that years from now

the soldier won't hear what he does now?
Who will plug the blackness the artist
has drawn for her mouth or tear off
her arms that wouldn't let go of her infant
that writhed like a bug in his hand for release?
Where does the soldier go after he is through

with this? What does he do through
the night to stop up his ears, which now
hear everything—and nothing? *Release
me,* the soldier's face seems to say. The artist
has the soldier look away from the infant
on his sword to the governor walking off,

whose back is turned, who's already off
to other matters because he's through
with this. For the governor, this infant

was an irritant he doesn't experience now
(the mother was something the artist
just didn't need to include). *Release*

her from her pain—or don't; release
yourself from whatever, or don't. Fuck off.
That's what his back tells the artist.
Whatever else happens, he's through.
It's of no concern whatever to him now.
In the history of warfare, name one infant.

The governor turns his back forever. Infant
death in war is propaganda, a news release
from the side that's losing. It's like that now;
it will be in the future. The powerful are off
to other business. They are already through
with this. That's what his back says to the artist.

In one final foreshortening, the infant hangs off
of the sword, releases the mother's hair, and reaches through
the plane as if the artist were now including us.

Masaccio's *The Expulsion of Adam and Eve from the Garden*

Brancacci Chapel, Florence, 2006

As Freud said, there are no accidents.
  For example, in *The Annunciation*
by Lippo Lippi, there's a glass that looks

out of place in that isolated spot
  in the painting's foreground,
but it's there for a reason. At the moment

the angel tells the Virgin she has been chosen,
  the light that enters her womb
penetrates the glass, and the glass is not broken.

I was reminded of this at my niece's
  graduation when my brother,
out of the blue, mentioned he has a photograph

of his daughter, taken when she was a tot
  with the last Shaker woman alive
in upstate New York. The old woman belonged

to that nineteenth-century sect started by a woman
  who believed the flesh was so hot
its heat could only be shaken off

in a kind of walking that produced trance.
        And there was no compromise,
not so much as a fig leaf was put over

the genitals' power to arouse. No, Mother
        Ann Lee demanded abstinence.
As their ranks thinned to bone fractures

and liver spots, the sect raided
        upstate New York orphanages
for the byproducts of others' lusts—

to refill the empty chairs now
        so admired in museums.
In April, I was in the Brancacci

Chapel. The fig leaf over Adam's
        cock was no longer there,
his genitals were not painted over.

I read in yesterday's newspaper
        that our casualties in Iraq have surpassed
twenty-five thousand killed and wounded.

Adam may have been delivered
        from the ideologically pure,
but the fresco says there's a lot more suffering ahead.

Piazza Shelley

Viareggio, Italy, where the corpse washed up

Shelley's bronze, mute, and young face
stares out over the piazza where his
is the only bust—just beyond, a bus is
waiting to pull out for Pisa or Florence,
maybe Lucca, because there's a concert
tonight by James Taylor and some group
I should probably know but have given up
trying (or even pretending) to stay current
about, and don't. There's no one here
except for a Muslim family—the woman
who appears to be guarding the empty stroller
as her husband hovers behind their son
past the inscription on the granite pedestal
which tells when Shelley drowned, and that's all.

Life Study

Viareggio bus station, Italy

He lifts him like they're wrestlers in the ring
or like in Pollaiolo's *Hercules*
and Antaeus, only neither of these
guys is a hero and both have been drinking
all morning—this isn't the Uffizi
and what they're doing isn't in a painting:
it's a park, James Taylor's going to sing
tonight in Lucca, people around me
are also waiting for their bus to swing
around that corner where, under the trees,
their drivers are on a break—but these
guys inhabit a sphere that has nothing
to do with music: the one whose back may bend in
half shoves a forearm into the mouth of a lion.

Head Games

Rome train station, summer 2006

Catullus, nothing's changed around Termini.
In the bars, drunks roll off of counter
seats like roasted meats off of altars,
and whores lining the wall at the Twistee
ice-cream stand always promise me
every time I pass through here
to buy a train ticket to somewhere,
if they can't make me cum, it's free;
and the police (always in pairs) eyeball me,
but wait until I buy the ticket, then saunter
up to demand my passport. I stare
at my photo, nervous, because I'm guilty
of something, and any foreigner who can't tell
that by now hasn't traveled.

Almonds

As I'm writing this, a woman on a cruise ship (not this one)
on her honeymoon, has gone over the railing of her cabin.

According to the TV news report, the husband said she lost
her grip trying to surprise him. He'd been next door

partying with a couple they'd met. White candy-coated almonds
were spilled all around the bridal patio deck. The husband

spilled his guts at first, then wouldn't say a word to reporters.
You see him (as cops duck his head into the back of their cruiser)

shouting back at the cameramen to *sod off* (yet the Greek police
appear bored). Watching the clip, you sense he's not some nice

guy that the gods or whatever decided to play some wicked
trick on (foreigner romances girl, five weeks later she's dead).

The in-laws, who never met him, aren't buying it for a second.
They say their daughter (and only child) was allergic to almonds.

I'm on vacation, heading to the shrine of Saint John Theologos.
I've read that during the Great War the smell of almonds meant gas.

Fur

While we were waiting for the uptown express
on the 34th Street platform, this woman
came up to my wife, not threateningly, simply,
with a purpose, as if she had something she
knew she had to do and was doing it
and my wife happened to be the object

of that single-mindedness, the object
being my wife's fur collar, whose express
purpose when her grandfather added it
decades ago was ornamental. This woman
was proving he was some tailor, though she,
of course, hadn't a clue. She was simply

coming over to touch the collar, simply
to take it between her fingers. I didn't object,
though she put me on my guard. She
wasn't threatening or anything, didn't express
some weird thoughts, didn't bark. The woman
saw the fur collar and wanted to touch it—

it looked like she'd had a hard time of it;
that's how she seemed to me. She smiled, simply,
like a little kid, the hand of this woman
stroking fur, then my wife, who didn't object
to a stranger touching her cheek or express
any kind of shock or fear, or anything. She

accepted the woman's touch. Maybe she
understood the woman's reason for doing it.
I didn't, whatever it was she needed to express
inside herself by coming up to a stranger simply
to stroke a fur collar. Today, fur is an object
for rage, or worse, but not for this woman.

As my wife and I watched this woman
brush her fingertips along the collar, she
was as gentle touching the fur as if the object
of her affection could respond, as if it
were alive. The woman did this, twice, simply
her fingers, back and forth, able to express

some need she simply had to give in to this once,
and it was enough. Once the object was attained,
whatever need it expressed, the woman walked off.

Brunelleschi's Dome

for Clo

The line's not long and she wants to climb
to the top of the dome and take pictures
of the horizon and everything below, and I tell her
that will have to include me because I'm not dumb
enough to think I can do that again—St. Peter's
was almost too much a few years ago. "Like iron,"
I answered when she asked me how my limbs
felt then—she said "limbs" because that was her
way of asking something else (about my ticker
quitting—once, it almost did). "Go on,"
I say after she asks me again. A dozen pigeons
scramble for the pieces of bread that she tears
off because she can't take the sandwich with her.
Then she's gone, and it feels like forever.

Faces

At Calvary Cemetery where I took the el
and then the subway to get home each day,
I'd cut grass in the old section where they
had photos in the headstones, white ovals
like ostrich eggs that had pictures of girls
inside them in white dresses as they prayed
the rosary—or, at the studio, posed that way.
I'd cut row after endless row. It was hell
and sometimes to kill time, I'd squat or kneel
behind a monument to get shade any way
I could, and there would be a whole family
looking back at me—portraits you could tell
were taken at the start of the last century
but might as well have been murals from Pompeii.

Ghazal

after eating at a greasy spoon in the university section of Padua

I had my guidebook, my map, my euros, and, most
importantly, time: in the window, a picture said "toast"—

a white-bread sandwich with brown grill-marks
striped across its surface—not what my head thought "toast,"

which once came from a bright, sleek, two-slice machine
like a miniature Airstream, which my dead father's toast

popped out of onto the Formica kitchen table
with its bent pipe legs—like his hospital bed—with toast

and crumbs and dark egg smear on his blue pajamas
that my mother wiped with a licked hankie. I said toast

but memory can be such a liar. It defrauds us. Not
crumbs—her scolding. The marriage was dead, toast—

with one too many visits to that VA psychiatric ward
in the Bronx when she repeated, "toast . . . toast . . . toast . . ."

Nighthawks

after Hopper

Three people sit at a diner counter
at night, lighted from inside: a man; beside him
a redhead, in a red dress, slim,
ready for action—anything—for the door
to open and someone to walk in, look her
over, sit on one of the stools at the end
of the counter, and give her a nod.
If someone half decent did, she'd be out the door.

The third figure, with his back to the viewer,
is hunched over his cup of coffee, the brim
of his fedora obscuring everything about him.
Bending over, the counter-guy is looking at her—
she's a hot one—as he dries a cup in his apron.
No one's leaving. The diner doesn't have a door.

Ghazal on NYPD Crime Scene Photos

1914–1918

We all think people are people and want to look their best in photos.
But look at these—they're no one anyone knows in the photos.

The police were pretty sure the murdered girl was a prostitute.
A young thing. Look how her killer posed her for the photo.

The tall, thin guy in the alley was from Harlem. Life was good.
He was stepping out. Take a look at his clothes in the photo.

The two-bit gangster slumped in the vestibule was always a curiosity.
Especially now. He was always suspicious of those in the photo.

The old woman lying face up in the basement next to the furnace—
the stream from the side of her head still flows in the photo.

And this one, taken at night, in a vacant lot, with a dusting of snow—
lying next to the small blanket, a doll's hair still blows in the photo.

Ghazal on a 1906 Murder Victim Photo

Lower East Side, NYC

The victim's in a hallway—this is the money shot.
Just like in porn, you don't miss the money shot.

He's on his back; there are eyeglasses in his hand.
You don't care if the glasses are his for the money shot.

He dropped his suspenders. His pants are unzipped.
There's a wallet. Was he getting a kiss at the money shot?

If he was getting off, it was tucked back into his pants.
It was different then with forensics for the money shot.

At left is a banister, behind it a stairwell (where someone
hid?)—you can almost smell the piss in the money shot.

Was he married? What about kids? What was his name?
There's no record of any of this with the money shot.

Ghazal on a 1914 NYC Crime Scene Photo

In this one, from Brooklyn, they all got sleepy in bed.
She's absent. She turned on the gas. There are three in bed.

The brother-in-law found this; he had to open windows.
He knew as soon as he entered what he would see in bed.

Her husband drowned the day before—he expected
the widow, his dead brother's wife, might still be in bed.

She wasn't. She was behind the door when he forced it.
When he stopped in the kitchen, he could see to the bed.

The ten-year-old's head never moved on the pillow.
He knew the boys were gone too if she was in bed.

These are faded details in pencil on a sheet from a notepad.
It was once attached with something gummy next to the bed.

Ghazal on a 1910 NYC Crime Scene Photo

It wasn't supposed to happen. Look over the room.
There are playing cards scattered all over the room.

But look at the booze bottles upright on the table.
They're also on shelves against the back wall in the room.

None of the bottles fell when it happened—just him.
A chair's over his head. That's an odd way to fall in a room.

It's like a statement—the chair's the period at the end.
Was he in too deep and someone said *call* in the room?

Or maybe he upset someone who was in over *his* head,
and a bullet was trump. There's a pall over that room—

it must have hung over many basement card tables.
A note says there were no eyewitnesses at all in that room.

Ghazal on a 1912 NYC Crime Scene Photo

Look at them all hanging out of those second-floor apartments.
You know there must be nineteen/twenty to each apartment.

It's night. They heard the commotion. Everybody's up.
There's a restaurant, a tailor, a grocery below those apartments.

Wine bottles, fabric bolts, bread loaves fill the shop windows—
the body's where you'd expect it to be in front of their apartments.

Everyone knows daylight's for people. You want animals in a jungle?
Go out at night, because that's where you'll be outside your apartment.

Now everybody's up, even crowding onto the sidewalk to look.
Someone should open his hand to see if there's a key to an apartment.

There's no street name or building number on the back of the photo—
just the area, as if everyone in Little Italy lived in the same apartment.

Ghazal on a 1916 Brooklyn Murder Scene Photo

This one's at the bottom of the stairs.
A basement. He left one shoe on the stairs.

There are two detectives: one's back is turned;
the other is looking up at you from the stairs.

His face says it all—victim's head smashed in
like a pumpkin—and he hasn't a clue on the stairs.

His partner may know something or have ideas—
we'd have to have a different view of the stairs.

Maybe he saw something; he's bending over.
Maybe he saw more than others do on stairs.

We'll never know. He's a blur. There are no notes.
We'll never know what anyone knew on those stairs.

Ghazal on a 1902 NYC Crime Scene Photo

labeled "The Gibson Girl"

There are two here. She's half off of the bed.
He's sitting in a chair at the foot of the bed.

He's not dead. He stares at the photographer.
Was she on the floor? Was she put on the bed?

At right is a fireplace with cat's paw andirons.
You can almost touch the soot from the bed.

Look at the corpse—you can almost smell her.
A poker's on the floor, a foot away from the bed.

He's an old man, four times older than she is.
Did he do this to her, then put her on the bed?

Look at that stare of his. Look at her scrolled hair.
She had a laugh as airy as a feather, or soot, in bed.

Ghazal on a 1915 NYC Crime Scene Photo of a Couple

Look at the pair of them in bed. Look at him.
That woman is not his wife. Shame on him.

Shame on her. She had a husband—he had a name.
If he walked in on them, who could blame him?

The lab would have examined the sheet under them
(they wouldn't be able to tell if she came with him).

That would have been the last thing either enjoyed.
Young, she would have wanted an orgasm, same as him.

Maybe that's why she had this other guy in bed.
Her husband's didn't work? That would shame him.

These are jottings in pencil on an attached envelope.
There's nothing else. It doesn't even name them.

Ghazal on a 1909 NYC Crime Scene Photo

labeled "rooming house homicide"

Sad—ten decades pass, and after all these years
that old woman still stares up from that bed.

Her mouth opens like a yawn. She's clutching
her bare left breast. She's bare on that bed

down to her waist, and the bottom of her dress
has been hiked up. On the stairs past the bed

through the open door, we see blurred figures
as the camera shutter opens in the air over the bed

and closes. That's the point of view in the photo—
the omniscient, looking down from somewhere to that bed.

Ghazal on a 1908 Murder Victim Photo

Morrisania Avenue, the Bronx

He's a grocer. Look at how everything mocks him.
He's still clutching his apron. Pain shocked him.

With all that blood, you'd think he was a butcher
but those are cans on the floor. He stocked them.

He was stocking them on the shelves behind him
when the perpetrator came around and blocked him.

Behind the counter, the grocer wasn't going anywhere.
When he turned around, that someone cold-cocked him.

And that was how it could have ended—money taken
from a till; his few possessions, hocked; and him—

but it didn't. Someone put a knife through that apron.
Then put the knife through it again. That shocked him.

Ghazal on a 1918 Murder Victim Photo

How do you drown on a rooftop in a wash basin?
Look at the naked guy. Look at the condition he's in:

there's crisp, dry laundry hanging overhead, a pulley
and a pole, but he looks hauled in from the ocean.

Soaking—one moment swimming, then hauled up
to rooftop tarpaper, still hooked through the chin.

Like he was a tuna. Which he resembles. A swollen
tuna that hard men watched gasping for oxygen

next to the wash basin, before someone clubbed him.
Then clubbed him again. On the back, there's a notation

in pencil on the photo (it's just one photo in dozens
and dozens of boxes): "unknown/ dock area/ Brooklyn."

Ghazal for Pretty Women and Venice

A water, a gelato, and a beautiful woman handing me change
near the Rialto Bridge wasn't something new in Venice.

Moments before, a mom held down her toddler's diaper for him
to pee into the Grand Canal—there's nothing out of the blue in Venice.

The kid's stream arced into the water like the stream
from a water god, but a god of something is always on view in Venice.

Or hidden—as in the mist rising out of the lagoon at morning
on the ferry to Murano, the gods may stay out of view in Venice.

Everywhere naked goddesses fly off to Mt. Olympus on ceilings in palaces;
you never know when a goddess may hand you a lunch menu in Venice.

Don't get me wrong—on the cab ride from the airport to our hotel
on the island, our driver, a young guy, was listening to 2 Live Crew
       in Venice.

It was unreal—on the causeway where lights seemed as distant as stars
over the black lagoon, Luther Campbell was telling everyone fuck you
       in Venice,

telling everyone about desire, rage, lust, race, cocaine, blow jobs,
and everything else censors in the States can't keep from you in Venice.

Our driver (who sang along beautifully in English), said Campbell,
aka Skyywalker, was a pioneer—you listened to what you wanted to
      in Venice.

He didn't understand Luther's obscenity arrest in Florida, the "Pretty
      Woman"
lawsuit, U.S. censorship, and other things I didn't have a clue about
      in Venice.

He said Italy should erect a bronze statue to Campbell instead of sending
her soldiers to die in Iraq. It was always on the news in Venice.

Impromptu on Titian's *Annunciation*

Church of San Salvador, Venice

White and black and red—three colors,
Titian claimed, were all he needed,
were all art needed: black darkens corners,
white illuminates, red is the lifeblood
that flows through the veins of the living
and gives figures the surface appearance

of flesh. In his *Annunciation,* the appearance
of the dove is iconic. That symbol colors
Christian perception—the god both as living,
physical creature and as spirit—and as needed
as the heart, in a vascular network, pumping blood.
The dove does seem pagan, but there's no corner

on symbolic use; no faith can claim to corner
that market. How to show spirit? Its appearance
is felt rather than seen—it's not flesh and blood.
So, like children, to good spirits we assign color;
to bad ones, darkness. (I guess what's needed
for any kind of belief is simplicity, since living

is difficult enough, and half the time, living
a lie, we push those feelings into corners.)
Look at this painting. Isn't what Titian needed

really an excuse to give his art the appearance
of virtue? Look at the Virgin. Look at her color.
She's a woman. Titian's a pagan. There's blood

in her. She's had periods, a teaspoonful of blood
followed by a torrent—with cramps—when living
with her would be hell. Look at that skin color.
That flesh is also mythic: she's Pasiphae in a corner
hiding the placenta, taken by a god who appeared
as a white bull she couldn't resist. But Titian needed

the Christian framework, just as his art needed
those three colors—that myth was his air, his blood.
He couldn't do without it, like other men then living.
That also explains why the angel's sudden appearance
doesn't stun her: the god's already had her, in a corner,
and gave her no choice. She's pregnant. Her color

shows us that. The divine needed a living womb again,
so her flesh and blood were given up in a corner—to a god
who appeared as a dove, shedding light, which contains every color.

Landscape with the Rape of Europa

after Minderhout, Museés des Beaux Arts

The god is all menace as he stands waiting
in the field for her, watching,
the switch of his tail brushing
flies away from his sheath and stomach. She'll bring

him flowers, lay wreaths over his shoulders
from crest down to his dewlap—
and he will pin her. The slap
of his scrotum will sound an alarm. All of her

handmaids will throw down their baskets and abandon
her. She will feel his hot breath.
Whether she experiences the "little death"
of orgasm that makes all mortals forget is irrelevant. The sun

will blind her. All of this he muses as if it were real
because what will be real is what he thinks.
As his hooves and pasterns sink
into the muddy grass, he shudders; his testicles

rise and descend in their leather pouch, phlegm
fills his nostrils as Europa—
who has no concept of the imminent future—
carries a basket to him.

Ghosts

I

I've come looking for the prison cell
        of St. Paul. The hole he was dropped into
is supposed to be around here somewhere, I tell

the guy selling bottled water and hand him a euro.
        The guy repeats, *no fizz,* points to the Forum
somewhere behind him, which I already knew,

and I say *gratzy* in my best American
        as I reach past a girl's bare shoulder for the bottle,
which is ice cold and drips onto her skin.

The guy doesn't have time. It's hotter than Hell
        in Rome in July, and the crowded Coliseum
next door, which I've just come from, swelled

with so many people between the columns
        it reminded me of the New York subway during rush
hour when I'd be waiting on the platform

coming back from my psychiatrist's office
        in lower Manhattan. (This was during the late Sixties,
and to escape the draft I'd joined the reserves;

a shrink was part of the conditions for my release.)
      I turn—the guy is hollering from a corner
of his trailer, jabbing a hand to the right for me.

II

I don't remember ever asking her
      about Rome, what she did, where she ate,
what hotel she stayed at, whether the monsignor

was good company, whether she had a private
      audience with the pope, which she would have wanted.
I never asked her, and now it's too late

to ask her anything. Already, she's been dead
      twelve years. The truth is, I've stopped missing her,
except occasionally. Sometimes I'll hear something said

that reminds me of her—especially laughter—
      which is odd, since I don't think of her as being
happy. Yet what I also often remember is a picture

of her in her hairnet and uniform and something
      on the stove that she's turning away from to greet
his eminence, who's come personally to bring

her the news that she's going to Rome to visit
      the Holy Father with him. That picture in the Chancellery
made the papers—my brother clipped one and framed it.

It hangs in his living room for everyone to see,
> and it's that smiling picture of her I remember
and that I never asked about her trip. What's wrong with me?

III

In some kind of photo shoot for a magazine,
> three gorgeous, leggy models in flimsy dresses
rush under a peppermint-striped tent between

takes where there's shade and food and drink. There's
> even an oscillating floor fan connected by cables
to a white van and generator that's filled the air

with its machine gun and gasoline smell.
> Don't get me wrong—*machine gun*'s a metaphor
for what the generator sounds like, that's all.

After some string pulling, I got out of one war.
> Not my father. He was infantry. After he came
home, he was in and out of psychiatric wards

and in the end he couldn't even say his name.
> At least, that's my aunt's version. My mother
wouldn't talk about him; I think she was ashamed

her whole life, and then I couldn't stop her
> when she came to visit me and my wife and her grandkids
the month before she died of liver cancer,

when what happened (or didn't) all got tangled

      up together in her mind as she tried to make some sense

of it—more for me, I think, than for her—but she wasn't able.

I was going to say this is strange. Fashion models who pose

      on marble ruins, keeping their wary eyes out for the cats

this place is notorious for—that's not strange. We know what is.

IV: Coda

A completely articulated fish skeleton in dust—

      head, tennis-bracelet spine, small half-barrel

of ribs, under which empty fast-food packets of some sauce

attest that this outcrop of ruin isn't just urinal,

      but also restaurant. And don't leave out fuck-palace—

the condom ring next to the glass shard with its label

of recent vintage. I'm at the ruin of the Three Graces

      where Rome's vestals were said to practice unusual

rites at night away from the prying eyes of outsiders. Such places

still have their uses.